EVEN THE SKIES ARE BLUE

Daniel R. Phen

ISBN 1-594899-97-5

This publication can be purchased from your local
bookstore or by contacting:
Muse Eek Publishing Company
P.O. Box 509
New York, NY 10276, USA
Phone: 212-473-7030
Fax: 212-473-4601
http://www.muse-eek.com
sales@muse-eek.com

Playlist

1	slam
2	Dads
4	stompin' the john
6	meth
7	road scene
8	candy store
9	Gang Boyz
10	Baby
11	Prelude
12	Interlude
13	knife I
	II
	III
16	News
17	the butler
18	Lisa M. P.
19	post season
20	gameday
21	goes to the runner
22	Red
23	scream
24	Moon
25	jumping
26	Memo Day Memorial
27	time
28	1/1/02
29	wee men
30	Strike Out
31	what shall I do?
32	Fathers Day
33	My Children / Daughter

For

Cassidy, Delaney, & Tierney
the glue that holds me together

Bruce & Jill
thanx for going beyond the next galaxy

Family
hey dudes, dig this

slam

I asked at the coffeehouse
about a poetry slam
and they asked
if I wanted to read
I said no
I want to compete
I want to cut
and devastate
local poesy poseurs
w/ their cute rhymes
kisses and cuddles
while I throw down
my jacket in puddles
waiting for the lovelies
to misstep and drown

to my point of view
I rule the spoken word
w/ force of personality
and this is my town.

Dads

I remember vividly
to this day
my father coming after me
tongue clenched in his teeth
as I ran crying and cowering
how he taught me the futility
of resistance,
my father
who trained me to be a coward.

I remember my mother
dancing madly in the background
screaming
      not the face, Russ
      this time please, not the face
and my brother
sobbing in fear
knowing next time
the lesson might be his to learn.

I remember Christmas morning
kindergarden for my brother
3rd grade for me
excitement waking me before dawn
I rouse my brother with Santa alert
we sneak into the living room
to look around and grab our stockings

back to my closet bedroom
with it's furnace rumble and waterheater red
pilot-eye
we made too much glee in discovery
kicking Dad awake from his Tom & Jerry
dreams
he strode into my tiny space
with vengence in his eyes and hell on his face
snatched little Jimmy from his place on my bed
drop-kicking him into the hall
where he ricocheted off the wall like a basketball
and this time I whimpered
like a puppy discovered in it's puddle

on this most holy of mornings.
Peace on Earth
Goodwill for schoolclothes
I celebrate by remembering Dad
mostly with his tongue clenched in his teeth
the master instructor
how he giveth then taketh away

stompin' the john

I hadda come down hard on the mope.
we was sitting on this retaining wall
drinkin' wine, doin' reds, shootin the shit,
when the john come by.
he coulda walked on,
but he just stopped front of me
and started talkin' like he knew us or sumpin',
it made my stomach turn over and start to sour
like he was a priest
or some fag teacher or sumpin'
well anyway,
I fuckin' hate when people start laughin'around me,
I always have,
and really did when him and my friends started up.
so I told him to kiss me.
his eyes got big,
as I jumped down off the wall
his mouth fell kinda slack, and he backed a step
away.
so I said come on cocksucker, kiss me.
he did this kind of nervous chuckle
and made a move for a coat pocket
when I swung with my whole fucking all.
he dropped to one knee,
groaning and holding his folded hands over his
face,
and I grabbed his hair
and started bouncing him off the sidewalk.
you shoulda heard him
wailing like a banshee.

4

It felt good
and I knew I was ruining his looks
and I did it anyway again and again
till he stopped moving.
I jerked him up for the crowds approval
and his face looked like fucking bloody screech-
ing hamburger.
I turned to grin at my friends
but there was only a big crowd of strangers there
now.
I turned back to go for his bucks,
but when the badge fell open in the wallet
I decided to leave it,
like quick.
I started to run and then it sunk in,
the noise I'd been hearing was the sound of
sirens
like from all sides.
as the crowd started to break-up in blue,
before I lost conciousness,
I remember thinking
oh God, it's all over
and I'm fucking dead now.

meth

you were busted
in a pickup truck
with your cash, computers,
credit cards and checks
8 months pregnant
high on meth
you can make it in the basement
sell it on the street
do it and you never grow fat
do it and you never die old
to local law you're scum of the earth
your Romeo Clyde Barrow
broke out a window
climbed down some bedsheets
at the county facility
his cellmate fell
busted hisself all to hell
gonna be stealin cars
and runnin' free

pregnant and jonesin
willing to die to get high
judge gonna fuck you up
take the kid
put you in the pen
and bury the key

road scene

punk kid burnin Nox
in his japped-up Accord
couldn't dial it down
quickly enough
to not become a rear bumper
on a F-150 Ford
so we all sat the curb
waiting for donut jockeys
to show up
write it up
let us go
finally
truckguy turns to the kid
says
go unhook that shit
they can't prove wax
kid says thanx man
I owe you a sixer
as he heads for his car
Fordman says make it a 12
I turn my head
to grin at his girlfriend

candy store

who make a move on the candy store?
glock braced bopperbangers
clusterbunch outside the door
cameras on the roof
cover alley & street
infrared & temp detectors
sense motion & monitor heat
weight alarm lockdown
on the first & second floor
electronic steelgate
push yo money thru hole in the wall
they count while you wait
so
who make a move on the candy store?
security better than county jail
there's no amnesty
& ain't no bail
just the buy & fly
we sell the gospel-got to have
ain't no credit
& no free ride
boys w/ Uzi's already tried
they be shit dumb
& they died
so
you sad bastards
who make a move on the candy store?

Gang Boyz

made sure to always
double or triple team you
as
more crowd in
to prevent escape
boy alone
had no defense
no excuse
or hope

they would circle slowly
talking in soft voices
teasing as they triangulated
picking their opening
moving in from behind
with kicks
ahead of punches
working kidneys and spine
before moving up
to face and head
with elbows and knees
conversing as they worked
offering advice
electric with power and knowledge
exploding with repressed sexual energies

    up they rep
    defeating foe
    they rule school
    they down, bo!

Baby

Baby gonna light you up
walk away unconcerned
if she pulls down it's X's
you're going home
      horizontal
severely tested
bested
busted
Babysized
w/ coins on eyes
She always packing
lethal heat
baby's pulse
is the heartbeat of the street
cut down 12 streetsweeper
Mac-10
or nines
she'll mow you like a Bowie knife
she got
a chrome hardballer .45
with a crosscut rubber grip handle
she gonna light you up son
then blow out your candle

Prelude

hieroglyphic treetops
hustlebump to the rustle
of night winds
in this slumbering city

stalking silently
suddenly aware
sound in summer darkening
rapid heartpulse
in T-Mile Park

revealing moonlight
shattered by overhanging branches
splinters eyeflash
spooks a thousand daring martyrs
to seek their haunted hideaways

a shine like the seashore
gleams like atrocities bones
this mysterious shadowface
in constant evolution
dares to intrude
paint this picture

         muscles ripple under
leather
         slicking echo of steel
stiletto blade
         off-pitch whine
         of someone singing
softly
a sherry serenade

         I move in closer

Interlude

hail sails
like bullets,
        in Thousand Mile Park,
short bursts,
then momentary calming.
I pull gloom around me as a cloak,
take a hit off the winebottle
and move out into the open.
the trees are sentinel,
        peering across the clearing,
                sifting the shadows
                        sealing my passport.

I smile,
dark
is close companion.
somewhere
the nitesiren's
chase a mother's son,
whisper the long goodbye.
clouds break-up over east thirty-sec-
ond,
and the moon
                winks a warning,
I'm over the wall
                and
                        away.

knife

I

whisper of leaves
light reflection
I pick up the knife
it is very sharp
cut very deep
someone could die
planning their move
never feel the stroke
too sharp
what's that warm on me?
wet warm pain
oh no! yeah!
could be tonight maybe tomorrow
I guess I'm ready
I listen to my surroundings
you can feel
when time is right
maybe tonight
the steel reflects, glints, dances
what are the chances
you & me
cuz I hate your guts
I found this knife
gonna do someone
do someone down

II

this guy was big
6'3" goin' 280
me 5'9", 180
him maybe 28 or 29
I'm 50 & feelin' it
every inch of carpel tunnel
every broken finger, toe, nose
ever
& he made it obvious
to everyone
he was gonna fuck-me-up bad
stomp me down for bein'funny
calling me bitch & shit
so we get outside
& when he turns around
I run up and hit him
twice left handed
with everything I got
square on the nose
& he don't go down
& he smiles through the blood
so I bring up the right
end this fight
messy like

what did he expect
a roll of dimes?

III

he came at me all wrong
knife in both hands
held high in the air
like some kinda ninja
when everything
everyone
every instinct tells you
get low
cut low
slice all the way up
get low with your body
move up & into the cut
go thru him
Fucking thru him!
but then
I broke my own rules too
cuz he rose so high over me
I dropped my blade
& grabbed his ankles
dumped him on his brain
one foot on his throat
the other kicking in ribs
singing
      testosterone
      bring it along
      or stay at home

News

I saw you
another time
in a different town
now
I see you here
not just happenchance
you know where I work
where I live
I've seen you on the street
on the way to nowhere you need to be
hanging where I hang
talking to people I talk to
standing at the bar observing
it ain't a meet someone kinda place
it ain't afterwork from nowhere
sometimes it's a note on the windshield
sometimes it's a lone ring of the phone
I see you with your camera
you ain't no tourist
probably a hidden tape recorder
probably never leave me alone
til I again step over the line
til I commit another crime
once ain't enough
a long enough stretch of time
so you hang where I hang
      a story worth dying for.

the butler

the butler went to the press
there was dna evidence
in the semen on her dress
he had no obligation to the family
his job was with the princess
by her side when she died
his confession included
that fateful ride
the butler went to the press
a million dollars
not a penny less
after the hospital
and police duress
he was approached by publishers
and he said yes
a pension plan of sorts.

Lisa M.P.

her father
was a food accident
or so I've always heard
that he was sitting
on the shitter
cheeseburger in one hand
ass wipe in the other
little Stevie on the radio
grunting and chewing
oozing cheeze everywhere
when his heart gave out
      King on the throne
returns to sender

post season

he been playin for shit
    here at Staples
wingin the wild one
reachin in
over the top
givin it up
not makin his stop
    flappin his lips
not liftin his hands
not shiftin his feet
    he's so complete
or so they said
    but his head's not in it
        his team is dead

game day

c'mon coach
do your job
it's the big game
the season's on the line
show some emotion
work for your team
the sidelines are your H.Q.
stalk and talk them
look people in the eye
let them know what you expect
breath a little fire
this ain't romance
work the clock
inspire the line
control the rock
refuse to die
wake up
climb down off that cloud
concentrate
if there's a moment
there's the hope of glory
      true story

goes to the runner

they said,
you can't get away
w/ that
around here,
and
the longer I stood there
the angrier
and more numerous
they became,
vocally over-whelming me,
pushing and threatening
so I
took off
the tie.

Red

She strolled the corner
but didn't look
that kinda girl
hadda real sweet smile
kinda innocent & dreamy
I hadda few bucks
so I thought what the hell
I'd give it a whirl
see if she partied
or wanted a cocktail
she saw me coming
and hit the corner
headed away in any other direction
smoking a cigarette & walking fast
red hair, red cocktail dress
red sling-back Jimmy Choo's
yeah I'm the kinda devil notices shoes
by the time I'd made the corner
she'd disappeared
a visage
is known by her cut
true love
is escape inevitable
                love mostly gone
                when most needed

scream

the scream of reality
woke me this morning
beating me up
and down again
with nightscares
and the following forboding
cold coin-operated hands
repeating ceaselessly overhead.
wondering what to do
& having the strength
facing down the trials
keeping promise
framing spirit guide
sacrificing
soldiering, scouting, marching
alert to everywhere
aware of everything
& nearly everyone
sneaking up behind you.
fantasy release me
from morning motel tv
mommy and daddy
gave me this gene
that made me ugly
made me obscene
pick up a drink
a chick
a smoke
leave off a loving relationship
with a song, punch, or joke.

Moon

moon is my best friend
for we both live alone
and have a lot in common
though I am flesh
and he is stone.
we work nights
and sleep by day
meeting before the dawning
for solitary cocktails
shared in intimate silences.
when isolation gets too difficult
I howl
when quiet weighs too much
he screams
both of us whisper your name
incantation
in the loveliest of dreams.

jumping

something's gone wrong
with mama's goldenboy
a bitter little seed inside
made certain all of merit died
is that alright God?
is that ok?
is there a reason
things turn out this way?
in your infinite wisdom
can you see a light
somewhere before me
burning bright?
something's gone wrong
you can feel electricity
quivering like a junkie
within me
        I love you Lord
for without you
I am wind
I have no-one
so throw wing over me
take me in
give me back
the missing puzzle piece

I'm afraid
to face your wrath
if what they say is true
and on my own
        falling stone
I come to you

Memo Day Memorial

somewhat short of breath today
maybe I'll expire tomorrow
feel somewhat sick today
guess I'll smoke a bowl
 today
 penned a charm
 cradling your name
 chanted choice lines
 twice
 reciting your name
 laid in the sun
 til stars had begun
yeah
you guessed it
 but they kept on
 and I felt kinda down
 like time spent apart
 was your pleasure train
 and my bloodgore
 dripping slowly d
       o
       w
       n showerdrains
today
bleeds desperately
into next year
from
I thought I knew you
to
it's dead
 adieu

time

the sky crashed down
the earth swallowed me
I the swaddled baby
unfamiliar w/ daylight
surrounded by comfort
lose my warm security
　　　now I smile
behind a hockey mask
happy Halloween
knowing the trick of treat
disguises sick
mine is hand that begs a stick
to strike away at hurts
but wait
time is heartdrum
pounding ever message
seeking cease
memories/ dreams/ wishes
mingle in whiskey haze
brazening out another morning
not yet
but soon
not when
but who and how
time
is a shotgun blast
a silent scream
a cold kiss
a train ticket

1/1/02

I bade farewell to youth
fondly and finally
after finding adulthood
to be horror clotted by truth
isolation
brings change
loss of confidence
discouraging sadness
so I journey
despondent at the wheel
making leap of no faith
warrior of lost soul
refusing to live in the world
that throbs as a nail in the brain
pledges with prostitute smile
      I'm gone
      I'm gone
so-long I've loved you
best I'm able
but this is beyond all bearing
promise
drank from reality
skull bowl
spat out darkness

wee men

we men
look for production
numbers don't lie
don't require intense detail
    we break it down
make it happen
close it out
no excuses
make it count
pick it up
sense of urgency
smarter than hard
hammer put to nail
plastic whatever cost
tack on a reasonable tip
goodbye
we gone

Strike out

wave goodbye to yesterdays
whistle an original melody
as you wander unmarked paths
greet each fork w/ unflinching eye
a search must open new doors
and still
these rules too will fall down.
to balance scales
between serenity & joy
it's not productive
to rehash the past
I do not advocate
we ponder or prevaricate
if at all possible
except in cases of courtesy
or lust.

what shall I do?

the dilemma
of trying to write
something intelligent
tastefully
w/ discernment
universal appeal
understanding
revealing
everything
w/out sounding wuss
draw focus from flaws
w/ verbiage that assuages
give pause to pain
sprinkle like rain
rhythmically
wound round jungle beat
pulsing pounding
pleasuring
intensively
this tingling elation
extends open arms
like treasure
toward
and beyond
mankind.

Father's Day

I was born to violence
had it beaten into me
at an early age
I learned the fun...
damentals of rage.
    saw sundog run
    sunbolt thru rain
    wind blow counterclockwise
    water spout from drain
    felt awe and wonder
    at sudden shocking abysmal,
and I beleive,
    there's a lake in heaven
    born of children's tears
    where flowers bloom
    in banks of flame.

My Children

my children
when they read my stuff
many years from now
might think me
wanton wastrel
slutish swine
when all this time
I'm celibate
appreciating past
that once was mine
adoration paying tribute
a devotion
singing the goodbye life.

Daughter

I love you
as you're sleeping
curled innocently into dream
parted mouth slight snore
like a kitten's purr
unfurled whisper
open to me
says in sleep I'm free
my elbows and knees
make room for me

7/4/03

Independence day
almost more than I can bear
July
4th year spent alone
independent
of a home
or family
detonations
and explosion
fill evening atmosphere
        w/ fountains, cannons, rockets
and missiles
the smallarms fire
erupts
dark sparkles
        so hot
                too dry
                        not your typical 4th of
July
just me
alone
choking on this dream I've chosen

they call me no-date-Saturday Nite
U-G-L-Y lookin for an alibi

I've been
damaged by a host of problems
indication etched upon me
like tribal tatoos
        and late
                the love comes down
till I'm childlike

afraid to talk adult to you

I stay alone

I stay alone
unworried about capturing love
making it mine
locking it in a house
binding it
w/ rules & laws
buying it
w/ flowers & gifts
weaving it
w/ friends & relatives
relationships
responsibilities
promises & vows
I refuse to know
this desperate necessity
that never perishes
      I stay alone

I don't know never

I don't know
where she got the idea
she could move
like me
if she moved w/ me
it wasn't happenin
and
I told her as much
but
she said I'd love it
if I gave it a touch
I
said I burned
at just the thought
it
went against everything
I'd ever been taught
I wouldn't
I couldn't
I'd never be caught

rain

unhappy
w/ your happiness
you wander off
to where
it's starting to happen,
a passage
from these depths
we've brought each other to.
sorrow
crushes chest
alters heartbeat
numbs limbs
drags blades thru braintissue
a cancer of sort.
how many scars
will you leave
on my nucleus
before it callouses over like leather
and too hard
dies.

for all the times
you've brought me pain
I wish you
rain.

the drop-dead poem

I'm sitting here
like
some kind of fucking Jack-o-lantern
hammering myself
into a post
while crazy blowing nightbirds
jazz around the outside
trying to bebop up the sun

kids on tv
cry out to the bronze lady
sing Our Country tis of Thee
& a streetwise
New York cop
shifts a sucker
to the otherside of his kisser
and asks
who loves ya baby?

I suck milk & rum tit
deliberating

Queen of hearts is wild
   somewhere in this downtown
   downshifting w/ her windows open
   wondering what's behind pulled shades
   listening for me
   intent on the music of my heart
   frantic
I'm not afraid to talk about this
I know there's a lot of you
who drink yourselves to sleep each night
arms crossed over chest
your desperation driving love
farther and farther away
asking fearfully
   who loves ya baby?

38

Ed & Ray

in the Whitney
Museum of Modern
Art New York New York
hangs Railroad
Sunset by Edward Hopper.
scarlet sky
below yellow gold
and violet
shot with plum
streaming cloud
streaking horizon. train below.

even though I never met him
I miss Raymond Carver,
and in his honor
I'm going to get drunk
before noon,
smoking
and staring out the window
see where the day takes me.

Your Father

has a Porsche Boxter
he keeps at a young girls house
he sugerdaddy's this sweet
    35 or 38 year old
but
while he's away
she's turnin' tricks
stashing aside a nest egg
plannin' her escape
to a paid for home on the Cape
    just another mil or two to go

she's taking him sure and slow
showing how it feels
the truth of youth
driving molten iron again
and a Boxter
she plans to take

boardboys on the beach
dig a convertable.

invulnerable youth

we knew
we would never grow old
we lived too fast
partied too hard
drove way too fucked up
    out where smokies guard
but
    we got caught
        from behind
            by corrosive old age
and frustrating erosion
    landscape dims
        we lose our vision
            concentration and conception
almost always sore somewhere
almost always tired
almost only 50 years
a lot of them hard
a lot of scars
to testify
I was callous and a fool

sorry
if I made you cry
I got too high
in my
    invulnerable youth.

god decides

don't
be afraid
of the darkness
within me
it's only
refracted light
God decides
whereon it rests
God
makes these choices
and laughing
         walks away
the onslaught
of love
is this that is left

like felt over the window
    obscuring reason

Jilly-

I am the blues
best you leave,
I don't want to live into the next.
amma rocker
wanna die before I miss anything.
n a hippie too
not to hurt you
or get in your way.
I thought,
to shine a light through your kitchen door,
but it ain't that no more.
          so say goodbye, bye,
I'm the highway
come 'n' gone.
somewhere down the road
you may accompany me again.
I didn't steal the Marc Chagall
I didn't lose it in the mail
I didn't hang it from a 16 penny nail,
museum-stickered back side out
for conversation sake.
I couldn't sell the Marc Chagall
no matter what you think of me
for smoke & drink as you suggest.
I'd be a lout, no!
It's much too beautiful
for such commerce,
I'd do the slam before I sing or sell.

Hell,
there were mornings
when sunbolt through bevelled glass
would turn the background
behind the silhouettes golden orange,
made 9:15 coffee time.
> you're so right
> it isn't fair,
> you give, I take,
> just a loser on the make.
> Ain't never gonna be right w/ me.
> I guess you're already gone
> in your heart
> you've done move on.
Some good guy gonna eat you up.

Dasn't

bend em knees

it's
an ebb and flow honey
like the motion of the ocean
back and forth
up and down
in and out
breeze in the trees
brushing the leaves
tighten release
open and close
heat and cool
fast then slow
its slow and go
pulse of life honey
          why
I love you so

now we're rollerskatin

desire dines

your ass in my chair
me on my knees
gnaw thru your underwear
bury my nose in you
abrade labia w/ facial stubble
mumbling somethings
as I slobber
slither
deliver
        your
fingertips
clutching pulling pleading
clenching & trembling
open & close
til breath escapes you
capturing abandon
quick flick lick
toward
another reckless element
        voracious
the tiger within
inhales your exclusivity
your electricity
& exists
solely in time
for this
your pleasure

playing

like children
playing under covers
  show me yours
  I'll show you mine
  I'm the doctor
  you're the patient
  you're the mommy
  I'm the dad
  you're the sugar
  I'm so bad
  if you let me
  you'll be glad
  do ya want to
  it's o.k.
everything will be alright
feel so wonderful
tonight
c'mon
let's

lgbd

little girl been dreamin
but...
it aint happenin,
she been fishin
hopin & wishin
but...
it aint happenin.
she brushes
and touches
smiles & blushes
but...
it aint happenin.

marriage

it's not something
I'd do for me
not out of hunger
not out of whimsey
not for attention
or camraderie
it'd be something for you
 not something for me

anything to think of

she awaits
neon sign
or in-flight movie
to appear
over my left shoulder
giving her
anything to think of
except
my breath in her ear,
a flash of lightning
thru
a far window
offers momentary relief
as I finish
and
roll away.

drams

when our hallucinations
have done their time
been released or pardoned
lived out squalid existence
flickered as candlelight
curtseyed and moved on to a new cowboy
been stomped under biker boots
fallen into precipice
last drop from the flask
played taps and lowered the flag
blown out the candles
turned off the light and closed the door
watched the last shooting star

when our dreams
leave this warm comfortable flesh
        hold jade in your hand
        for the broken heart
no promise is forever
just a closing eyelid
click of a shutter
held breath
forever promised moment of love
gone

chance to start again

corner of the heart

there's a corner of the heart
where dreams are born
near take a chance-
make a friend
over by the rainbow's end
cornucopia
where hopes are seeded,
sun shine's on thought
and nature takes.

let us leap
logical bonds and boundaries
to free frolic far beyond flight
where melody and sight
reverberate passion,
warm scent
from scooped hollow of your throat
implicates kisses unending.

in dream
we waltz hand in hand
into darkness
deeper, longer
among the small spaces
where sparks of memory
make you tremble
at discovery.

my gaze is destiny
my smile your future
touch surpasses bliss
there is no spoken word possible
only honey,
this corner
where you live.

perhaps

perhaps
if I could
keep my eyes off you
if I could
control my tone of voice
my trembling hands
disquise
desperation & longing
be as false
as reality t.v.
I might impress you
sincerely
charming as could be
confident & cruel
imprison you
with desire and expectations
direct and erect
proud to run up standard
be the eternity
you counted on.

I expect

I
expect nothing from you
wish
everything for you
it is enough
to know there is you
lightens my burden
gives hope where there was void
I
will do for you
beleive in you
have faith in you
trust
in the magic of you
see purity
with perfect clarity
everytime
I dream you mine

one-night

I'm the one-night stand
you never forgot
I remember you too
your satisfaction was my pleasure
your smile
fluttering eyelids
& whispered words
are personal treasure
safely locked away
gallery
& if ever
we meet again
amongst myriad somedays
well, who knows?
til then
godspeed

down

I'm celibate
like a stone
time passes
rain washes me down
& down I'll stay
tears are redundant luxury
I allow myself no penance
except occassional loss thru theft
your brothermine bleeds me
a purification leech
we are & call ourselves society
recent lack of morals
amongst acquaintances disturbs me
recent lack of desire
disturbs me
the girl next door
existing no more
somehow I doubt love
happening for me
      I'm celibate
      like a stone
      washed long down
      longing for the sea

Eulogy
(rhyme for a time & place)

nite eyes
cry ice
sirens of evening wind
weep silent psalms
moan visions of longing
futurity's chill blue breath
stealing secretly savagely
plants a dagger of suggestion
from phantom passion
fragrance wafts warning

   your kisses summerwarm
   touch home center
   scale emotion heights
   sail happiness kite
   the contact enterprise
   blossomed in forest & field
   left this raging river
   of I want you's
   rushing to heartache
   neath sobbing stars

   alone
in filthy rooms
with desperate quiet
a humble cloak
misery sat with oath unmuttered
drinking hard of damning sentiment
toasting agony sacrament
useless writhings
penance writings
dream altar prayer

  the dead are doomed
  to endless dark
  without morn
clouds absorb my tears
with silent sighs
& too soon spill

  the song stillborn

heart of rain

a childlike laughter was ours
nourishment entertainment peace
someone somewhere stole it
     when will you lay in my arms?

teasing the c

somedays
blood pours from me
in 5 gallon buckets
but still
I hop aboard
the back of the beast
for one last ride
     to drink from the water
     is to swallow tide.

hypnopompic

love making
satiating
& rest
wickedly happy
before dining
passionfruit & flaming wine
savoring sup
moist lips on moist
into dankly sweet dusk
where shines only
light of perhaps
humming softly as she blows sorrow away
     someday it will all be yes

calling card

you are my darling
     and evening's quintessence.
the moon is but half-light
     glistening on your aura.
I sip,
     sitting in mute concentration,
          life is indeed
wonder!
The Dancer-
     (renowned for dusky corners,
      and dipping hands)
at your service,
in fact my darling,
     at your command.

kiss

let us linger awhile.
the tide ebbs toward sunset,
blending light with motion,
angle with degree.
the measure of a moment.
sea's salt breath stinging,
a kiss known forever
without age or memory.

the very small fire

she may have kissed you back
throwing her arms around your neck
stared questioningly into your eyes
sealing a friendship
beginning a relationship
willing the dream
hope melting one's breath into another

wanting to protect you
respect your precious desires
my kiss but brushed your cheek
smiling we did not speak
a lingering thought
planted in the garden of possibility

    did you think of me
    before you slept?

river of love

I imagine you
bathing in warm soapy water
your breasts floating free
winking
in and out of bubble prisms
as I slowly
reach my hand
into the bath
to find the beginning of you
and make you gasp
      your head lolls back
      your eyes close slightly
now I have your attention
we share this slippery moment
create our history.

erecting memory
of artificial monuments.

bruise

this
is what makes me feel good
this
like from the heart
this
harkening back
hope & memory combined
a now composed
of thens
      future & past
innocence on the wind
the goodness in you
pleasure it sends me
wave ebbing bon jour au revoir
a warming soul
in a cooling atmosphere
thanks you madly

vision

I dream
w/out sleeping
     you materialize
behind my closed eyes
again I escape
     make way to you
surround you like sea
whisper you
     breeze in autumn fields
drink you fresh icewater
breath you
everything you
wherever, however
in first mystic awakenings
press my face to you
forest floor pillow
absorbing frost flavor
     hill to valley echo
alders & birch go gold
waterfall hair cascade
over my armbluff
secure you
     tongue taste you silver
in moonlight bathed
paint winking eyeglint
upon soft swell of mounding flesh
under work worn hand
throaty sound of voice
trying to elucidate
I wait
turn to the wall
and sleep

You

I celebrate you
take joy in you
lo I have loved you
these many years
thru flame
fury
ecstasy
despair
tasting the light of you
inhaling your essence.

embrace

this is me
when I cry for you
this is me
as I cry out your name
and I as butterflies
drop from my swollen eyes
promise portent
the marvel of we
eyes closed
lips swollen
eternal fantasy
momentarily

compass

I
just can't see you
without my heart leaping
like speckled trout
in Montana stream
unyeilding
willing my way
onward
unsure but influenced
by the wave of your hair
the turn of your face
tenderness of your voice
tremble in your lip
starfall in your eyelight
and everything
points me
towards you
like the North Star
points home.

Li, Edgar and I

it was billed
as the world's most dangerous poem
and I was afraid of it.
all the details it might reveal
names named and addresses quoted,
there's nothing more powerful than
truth
and truth will set you free,
set you aflame.
we walk into radiant light
but I desire no transport,
don't want to know
don't want to hear,
one of too many poems
that intimidate and cut.
my flower is auto rust
mixed w/ red clay dust
I like to hang & chill,
slow mambo before I twist
I make slow magic
not a flick of the wrist.

I hope
the scenes I strive to capture
become clearer
more succinct
as I grow blind & deaf
the kid who's just been kissed
missed a lotta stuff
the first time around.

trying to home in on warmth and
honey
cuz
there's been many dark alleys,
blind dead ends
poems that insinuate
or peter out
or left you pissed or frozen.

so
I'm out
on this corner
huddled over this trashfire
notepad out
scribbling about something I heard
and passing a bottle of red
with Edgar Allen & Li Po,
cuz they know.

if ever

if ever you love me
sums of us would equal
water lit by moonlight
sunbright breeze upon the heath
time precious teardrop

stop

momentarily
my memories
touch
reluctantly
upon now
and back to then

www.ingramcontent.com/pod-product-compliance
Lightning Source LLC
Chambersburg PA
CBHW021911040426
42447CB00007B/799